Pope Gr

By Unit

https://campsite.bio/unitedlibrary

Table of Contents

Disclaimer

This biography book is a work of nonfiction based on the public life of a famous person. The author has used publicly available information to create this work. While the author has thoroughly researched the subject and attempted to depict it accurately, it is not meant to be an exhaustive study of the subject. The views expressed in this book are those of the author alone and do not necessarily reflect those of any organization associated with the subject. This book should not be taken as an endorsement, legal advice, or any other form of professional advice. This book was written for entertainment purposes only.

Introduction

Delve into the life and complex legacy of Pope Gregory VII, an enigmatic figure who left an indelible mark on the Catholic Church and the course of history. In this meticulously researched biography, the multifaceted persona of Hildebrand of Sovana comes alive, tracing his transformation into Pope Gregory VII and his tumultuous reign from 1073 to 1085.

Renowned as a great reforming pope, Gregory VII's influence was felt across the corridors of power in both the ecclesiastical and political realms. His pivotal role in the Investiture Controversy, his fiery disputes with Emperor Henry IV, and his unwavering assertion of papal supremacy and authority reshaped the landscape of medieval Europe.

Unfolding against a backdrop of power struggles, spiritual fervor, and ideological clashes, this biography uncovers the nuances of Gregory VII's character. From his rigorous enforcement of clerical celibacy to his confrontations with simony and his bold excommunications of Henry IV, his actions were both audacious and divisive. His complex relationship with the Church's history, his contemporaries, and the larger socio-political landscape is explored with meticulous attention.

Gregory VII's enduring influence, even after his death, is illuminated through the contrasting narratives that emerged in later generations. From charges of necromancy and torture to admiration for his moral force and religious conviction, his legacy is a tapestry of reverence and criticism. This biography offers a comprehensive exploration of a pivotal figure whose imprint on the Catholic Church and Western history resonates to this day. It invites readers to engage with the intricate interplay of power, faith, and ambition in the life of a saintly yet controversial pope.

GREGORIVS VII.

GREGORIVS . VII . PAPA . SAONENSIS

Pope Gregory VII

Gregory VII, born Hildebrand of Soana (Soana, c. 1015 - Salerno, May 25, 1085), was the 157th pope of the Catholic Church from April 22, 1073 until his death.

Sent very young to study in Rome, he came into contact with the values of the Cluniac reform probably through the teachings of Lorenzo d'Amalfi and Giovanni Graziano, the future Pope Gregory VI. He became, under Pope Leo IX, papal adviser and began to exert a very strong influence, so much so that it has often come to be referred to as the "Gregorian reform" to indicate that transformation taking place in the church of the time. On April 22, 1073, he was elected pope by acclamation, without following the prescribed canonical norms, prompting criticism regarding legitimacy that would persist throughout his pontificate.

During his pontificate, Gregory VII spent vigorously in combating simony, Nicolaism, and, above all, in affirming papal primacy over secular power. Probably in 1075, he wrote the famous *Dictatus papae*, a series of 27 statements concerning rights and prerogatives that in his intentions were to be attributed to the pope. His firm intention to take the right of investiture away from the secular power led him to a clash, which has gone down in history as the "investiture struggle," pitting him against the king (and future emperor) Henry IV of Franconia, the latter wishing, instead, to restore imperial authority. The struggle resulted in dramatic and unprecedented events, with Henry going so far as to dismiss Gregory and the latter responding by excommunicating him. Emblematic was the so-called "humiliation of Canossa" by which the young emperor intended to ask the pope's forgiveness.

The struggle ended negatively for Gregory, who was forced in 1080 to flee Rome and take refuge in Salerno through the protection of the Norman Robert Guiscard. Gregory would die in exile in 1085, however, his dogged action had by then deeply impacted the Church and changed the power relations with the temporal power. Considered one of the most important popes in history, he unquestionably contributed to forming the structure of the Church that essentially remains to this day, fostering the process of transformation that led it to shape itself as a theocratic monarchy with centralized power. The cult paid to him since his death was ratified in 1606 by Pope Paul V, who proclaimed his sanctity. His liturgical memorial is May 25.

Historical context

Pope Gregory VII was born at the beginning of the 11th century, when the Western Christian world was reaching the height of a period of relative political stability and cultural growth, known as the "Ottonian Renaissance," and economic development framed in the so-called "year 1000 revival." The emergence of the Ottonian dynasty with Otto I of Saxony, crowned emperor in 962, had strengthened the centralized power that had broken down with the breakup of the Carolingian empire following the Treaty of Verdun in 843. Otto I's successors, Otto II and Otto III, had pursued the ideal of *renovatio Imperii* without, however, being fully successful. Despite the authority the Ottonians were able to impose, European society still remained strongly based on the feudal system, characterized by a fragmentation of power centers. The political situation had not changed much even with the advent of the Salic dynasty, which ascended the imperial throne in 1027 with Conrad II the Salian. If in Germany the king ruled by sometimes having to face the various local princes, who were often very powerful, in the meantime southern Italy had recently been conquered by the Normans, while in the kingdom of France since 987 the Capetian dynasty had been established, which in Gregory's time ruled over a much smaller territory than in present-day France. In England, in 1066, William the Conqueror had instead wrested the island from the Anglo-Saxons.

From birth to pontificate

Family origins

Few and uncertain are the data on the origins and social status of the family of the future Pope Gregory VII. It is known for certain that he was born in Tuscany, in Sovana, on an unspecified date but probably to be placed between 1015 and 1020. His baptismal name, Ildebrando, testifies to the Germanic origin of his family, which seems to have been of modest background and, according to some sources, undoubtedly intent on showing some parallelism with Jesus, his father, a certain Bonizone (or Bonizo), is said to have practiced the profession of carpenter.

Training

The context in which Hildebrand grew up was characterized by a real moral crisis in the church (a period known as *saeculum obscurum*), which had long been discredited by the practice of buying and selling ecclesiastical offices (known as simony) and the spread of concubinage or marriage for clergy members (nicolaism), situations that were frequent particularly in Italy,

Germany and France. In response to this situation since the end of the 10th century, a profound reform of the church had begun, initiated in particular by the monastic world, which aimed to obtain greater autonomy from lay power and to impose a moralization of conduct, both of the clergy and of the class of chivalry, thanks to the initiatives of God's peace and, later, God's truce. The reform movement was largely supported by the Cluniac congregation (originating from the abbey of Cluny) but not only: also leading the reforms were the Benedictine abbeys of Brogne in Belgium and Gorze in Lorraine (famous for the Gorze Reformation).

Hildebrando was sent very young to study in Rome where his uncle was prior of the Cluniac abbey of Santa Maria on the Aventine, reformed in the 10th century by Oddone of Cluny at the behest of Alberic II of Spoleto. Here Hildebrando began his ecclesiastical training, becoming, almost certainly, a monk. His teachers included Lorenzo d'Amalfi and most likely also John Gratian, future Pope Gregory VI, an ardent supporter of the reform. The instruction given to the young man was mostly mystical rather than philosophical; he drew more from the psalms or writings of Pope Gregory the Great (whose name he and his master would assume once they became popes) than from, for example, those of St. Augustine.

Chaplain of Gregory VI

When Gregory VI ascended to the throne of St. Peter, the young Ildebrando was given the post of chaplain to the pope. The pontificate that followed was particularly turbulent and ended with the military intervention of Emperor Henry III of Franconia in Italy, who, on December 20, 1046, at the synod of Sutri removed the pontiff, accused of simony, to impose Pope Clement II in his place. The following year Ildebrando followed the now-deposed Gregory VI into exile in Germany and remained with him until his death in 1048. Although he had not been fully persuaded to leave Rome, the stay in Germany proved to be of great formative value to Hildebrus, proving crucial to his later ecclesiastical activity.

Adviser to the popes

Meanwhile, some controversial events had taken place in Rome: in quick succession, the two popes appointed by the emperor, Clement II and Damasus II, had died. When, in 1048, Brunone of Toul was proclaimed pope, Hildebrand persuaded him to take off his episcopal robes and travel to the capital of Christendom as a simple pilgrim, asking the clergy and people for renewal and confirmation of his appointment. The Romans welcomed this show of humility, and Brunone was able to be elevated, on February 1, 1049, to the papal throne with the approval of all, assuming the pontifical name Leo IX. At the explicit request of the new pontiff, Ildebrando was invited to return to Rome, which he did in 1049, albeit unwillingly, beginning a career that would lead him to be one of the most influential churchmen.

In fact, shortly after his election, he was appointed subdeacon, receiving the task of administering the finances of the Holy See, which at that time had fallen into a disastrous situation. Thanks to this assignment, he was able to exert considerable influence over the pope, so much so that historians have often pointed out that the most important acts of Leo IX's pontificate were carried out only as a result of his advice. Hildebrando's influence did not end with Leo's death but continued to be an influential adviser to his successors as well. In this way he was able to be one of the leading figures in the ongoing reform, so much so that some historians would later call it the "Gregorian reform," twenty-five years before he himself became pope. Thanks to his advice, the organs of papal government were reorganized on the imperial model, and cardinals were entrusted with numerous important positions; moreover, the college of cardinals, once reserved exclusively for members of Roman noble families, was also opened to "foreigners," demonstrating the universal character of the Church and, at the same time, removing such appointments from possible buying and selling.

In 1054 Hildebrand was sent as papal legate to France to investigate the heresy of Berengar of Tours who claimed that there was only a spiritual presence of Christ in the Eucharist. Berengar was referred to the Council of Tours in 1055, presided over by Hildebrand himself, at which he decided to make a profession of faith where he recognized the transubstantiation of bread and wine into the body and blood of Christ.

Leo IX died in 1054, and a Roman delegation to which Ildebrando also belonged went to the German imperial court to conduct negotiations for the succession, succeeding, in view of the *Privilegium Othonis*, in convincing Henry III of the Holy Roman Empire to choose Gebhard of the Counts of Calw, later known as Pope Victor II, as successor. In this way the Reform party thus remained in power in the Holy See, although the pope continued to be appointed by the emperor. Following Henry's death, his young son of 6 years was elected emperor under the name Henry IV of Franconia, however, the temporary regency of Agnes of Poitou, widow of the deceased, was imposed. Although the latter was close to the Cluniac movement, her weakness caused difficulties for the reformist cause as she had to submit to the influence of the nobles who forced her to appoint as prelates people indicated by them.

When Victor II died, Pope Frederick of the Dukes of Lorraine (Stephen IX) was elected in 1057 without prior consultation with the German imperial court. Ildebrando and the bishop of Lucca, Anselm, were sent to Germany to secure his, albeit belated, recognition. Stephen IX's pontificate was short-lived, however: he died before Ildebrando's return and, with the hasty election of John Mincio (antipope Benedict X), bishop of Velletri, the Roman aristocracy made one last attempt to regain lost influence. Overcoming the crisis was essentially the work of Hildebrand, who succeeded in gaining support from the powerful noble Goffredo il Barbuto, who allowed the entry into Rome of a legitimately elected pope in the person of Gerard of Burgundy, bishop of Florence, under the name of Pope Nicholas II. Hildebrando's influence can also be attributed to two important political directions, which characterized the pontificate of Nicholas II and guided the Holy See's actions during the following decades: rapprochement with the Normans in southern Italy and alliance with the pauperistic, and consequently anti-Germanic, movement of the Patarini in northern Italy.

Among his first acts, the new pope had the papal bull *In nomine Domini* promulgated, which transferred the election of the pope to the College of Cardinals, thus taking it away from the nobles and people of Rome. Historians speculate that the actual author of this decree was actually Hildebrando himself. Also during this period, Hildebrando was appointed abbot of St. Paul Outside the Walls, a title he would retain even after his election as pope. Historians agree on Ildebrando's strong personality, described as one for whom "there were no nuances, but only *aut-auts*, black or white, and his brusque character won him few friends," but without forgetting his fervor and passion for religion and his full adherence to the reform to which he dedicated his life. His abilities to influence his surroundings were also well recognized by his contemporaries, the theologian Pier Damiani for example described him as "a worthless iron, however, like a magnet, capable of dragging behind him everything he encounters," or, again, as "a tiger about to take a leap, or a stiff north wind."

When Nicholas II died and was succeeded by Alexander II (1061-1073), Hildebrand increasingly appeared as the soul of curia policy in the eyes of his contemporaries.

The election to the throne

On the day following the death of Alexander II on April 21, 1073, while the funeral was taking place, the Roman people acclaimed Hildebrand as the new pope, and on the same day he was taken to St. Peter in Chains and legally elevated by the cardinals present to the pontifical dignity, with the pontifical name of Gregory VII. This mode of election, not provided for in the *Decretum in electione papae* issued a few years earlier, was to be bitterly contested by Hildebrand's opponents, particularly Guibert of Ravenna (future antipope). Gregory also did not write to King Henry IV of the Romans to notify him of his election, not wanting, therefore, to recognize the temporal power's right to control papal election. On the following May 22 the new pope received priestly ordination and on June 30 episcopal consecration.

The pontificate

Throughout his pontificate, Gregory spent himself pursuing the reform of the church, combating what he saw as the major problems afflicting it, namely, the widespread habit of clergy to marry or practice concubinage ("nicolaism"), the buying and selling of religious offices ("simony"), and the custom of episcopal investiture (the selection and appointment of bishops and abbots) by the secular power; the struggle against the latter led him to a fierce clash with Emperor Henry IV of Franconia. The vast epistolary left by Gregory VII (438 letters) illustrates what principles guided his reforming action from the beginning and are the fundamental historical sources for reconstructing his pontificate. Most of these letters, sent by Gregory to the powerful of the time, to religious and monastic communities and to civil communities, are preserved in the *Registrum to* which must be added those called *Epistolae vagantes*. Following are some excerpts:

If the decadence of the Church had also been determined to a good extent by the appointment of unworthy bishops, chosen only on the basis of the contribution paid to the royal or imperial coffers, it should not, however, be concealed that this was also due to the pusillanimity of the good guys:

Here, therefore, is the duty to promote different behavior, on the one hand encouraging bishops and abbots to oppose simoniacal practices, and on the other urging kings and high feudal lords not to extort money: this is the content of many letters in the epistolary. It was also necessary to set a good example, that is, to sustain a tough confrontation with the young king of the Romans Henry IV, who was surrounded by excommunicated bishops and aware that his father had deposed and elected more than one pope. Gregory had no difficulty in assessing the danger:

Struggle for ecclesiastical celibacy

Among his first initiatives, Gregory VII, fought against Nicolaism, or the frequent practice of clergy to marry or practice concubinage. Hildebrand considered ecclesiastical celibacy inextricably part of the priestly ideal, deeming it essential for clergy to be dedicated solely to the church, without the distractions of a family and social ties. In the Lenten synod of 1075, Gregory VII went so far as to stipulate that a presbyter, whether regularly married or concubinary, should be relieved of the performance of his ministry and deprived of any ecclesiastical benefits until he did penance and changed his lifestyle by accepting celibacy.

These dispositions received challenges from many German priests, and the embarrassed bishops, especially in Germany, showed no promptness to put the council decisions into practice. Therefore, the pope, doubting their zeal, ordered the dukes of Swabia and Carinthia to forcibly prevent the rebellious priests from officiating. He was then reproached by bishops Theodoric of Verdun and Henry of Speyer for weakening episcopal authority before secular power by such a decision. At first, Emperor Henry IV, already busy facing the revolt of his great feudal lords, tried to calm the conflict by offering to act as conciliator between the papal legates and the German bishops.

In Spain, under pressure from the papal legate, the Council of Burgos in 1080 ordered married priests to renounce their wives, but this provision would not be put into practice until the 13th century during the reign of Alfonso X of Castile in which priestly marriage was severely punished.

In France and England things proved even more difficult. The synod of Paris in 1074 declared the Roman decrees intolerable and unreasonable ("*importabilia ideoque irrationabilia*"), and although the council of Poitiers in 1078 accepted Pope Gregory's provisions, the bishops could hardly put them into practice, as they lacked the indispensable support of secular authorities, and so interchurch marriages continued. Across the Channel, William the Conqueror did nothing to enforce the reform, and Lanfranc of Canterbury could not prevent the Council of Winchester from authorizing married priests to keep their wives in 1076. The council of London in 1102, under the inspiration of Anselm, ordered the annulment of marriages but without prescribing sanctions. The second council of London, held six years later, had no result other than to aggravate moral disorder in the clergy.

Investiture struggle

The phrase **investiture struggle refers to** the clash between the papacy and the Holy Roman Empire that lasted from 1073 until 1122, concerning the right to invest (i.e., to appoint) high ecclesiastics and the pope himself.

During the Middle Ages investiture was an act by which, through a rite called homage, a lord, the *senior,* conferred on another person, the *vassus*, a possession or right, the *beneficium.* In the 11th century, secular rulers considered it their prerogative to appoint bishops and abbots of their choice, and thus invest them spiritually, as a consequence of having entrusted material goods to them. Such custom gave temporal power supremacy over spiritual power, and this had resulted in a profound failure of the clergy to perform their function.

The first movements aimed at gaining greater independence for the Church occurred as early as the early 900s within the monastic milieu, but it was in the following century that real reform spread throughout the Church. The culmination of said reform occurred during the pontificate of Pope Gregory VII (begun in 1073), who, a fervent supporter of papal primacy above any other power, came into harsh conflict with Emperor Henry IV of Franconia, initiating the struggle for investiture. The clash had serious and unprecedented implications, with the emperor going so far as to order the pontiff to resign his position and the latter, in response, going so far as to excommunicate and depose the former. Famous is the journey Henry undertook in 1077 to ask forgiveness from Gregory VII, host at that time of Countess Matilda of Canossa, so that he would remove his excommunication and thus restore the duty of obedience on the part of his subjects, who had already been raised against him. Gregory's pontificate ended in the worst way, however: an antipope, Clement III, was elected, while the pontiff died in exile in Salerno under the protection of the Norman Robert Guiscard.

The confrontation persisted even with the successors of Gregory VII, ending in 1122, when Pope Calixtus II and Emperor Henry V came to an agreement with the signing of the Concordat of Worms. The agreement stipulated that the choice of bishops would fall to the Church and that they would then take an oath of allegiance to the secular monarch; the exclusive right of the Holy See to invest ecclesiastical offices with sacred authority, symbolized by the bishop's ring and pastoral staff, was being affirmed; the emperor, on the other hand, retained the right to preside over elections to all high ecclesiastical offices and to arbitrate disputes. In addition, the emperors of the Holy Roman Empire renounced the right to choose the pontiff.

Relations between the Empire and the Church between the 9th and 11th centuries.

During Charlemagne's empire, civil power was strong, and bishops again came to be regarded as mere functionaries, over whose appointment sovereigns could interfere heavily. As a result of the political instability following the breakup of the Carolingian empire, the Latin Church, and in particular the institution of the papacy, went through a period of severe decline known as *saeculum obscurum*. Corrupted by power struggles, Peter's throne became prey to local factions, thus discrediting its spiritual mission. In an era marked by a waning of central power, the political system that came to be established was feudalism, based on a reciprocal relationship between a lord (*senior*) who attributed a material good (*beneficium*) to one of his vassals in exchange for loyalty and aid; this system went, inevitably, to be reflected in ecclesiastical offices as well.

When, in 936, Otto I of Saxony became king of Germany (and emperor from 962), he systematically based his political power on assigning important civil powers to the bishops he appointed. Since they could not have legitimate offspring to whom he could pass on the benefits, a situation was established that was only temporary, since upon their death the crown would reclaim them. The first powers they were given were those of *districtus*, that is, of command, police and collection over the city and the immediately surrounding territory. Although this administrative system was peculiar to Germany, close links between spiritual and temporal power were also established in France, England and Spain. This consolidated the custom of the king appointing bishops and abbots, a practice that was nevertheless widely accepted by society since the monarch was seen not as a mere layman but as a lord chosen by God and thus fully legitimate in intervening in the affairs of the Church.

Therefore, under Otto I and his successors in the Ottonian dynasty, the bishops of the *Reichskirche* (literally "the imperial church") represented the foundation of the imperial administrative system; their investiture was symbolized by the handing over of the ring and pastoral staff by the emperor to the appointed bishop. This practice affected not only dioceses but also royal monasteries and large secular chapters. The coming to power of the Salish dynasty in 1024 with the election of Conrad II changed nothing in this organization, which persisted until the reign of Henry III (1039-1056). Monasteries and bishoprics thus became centers of even economic power throughout Europe, and no ruler could relinquish control over the appointments of bishops and abbots.

With such a system, the bishop's function was distorted by it, because the awarding of the office was no longer based on the candidate's moral gifts or religious culture, but solely on his personal loyalty to the emperor. The practice, moreover, quickly degraded into simony, that is, in giving the episcopal title to those laymen who were able to pay substantial sums of money to the emperor, certain to recover them later through the feudal benefits that now accompanied the appointment.

The reform of the 11th century, the role of Henry III the Black

This situation inevitably clashed with the religious ideals of some men who proposed, instead, a Church closer to Christian ideals and detached from the influences of secular powers. The first reform movements, inspired by the thought of Benedict of Aniane, took place from the first half of the 10th century in the monasteries of Lotharingia and especially in the abbey of Cluny in Burgundy, founded in 909. The latter had the particular characteristic of enjoying, thanks to its founding act willed by William I of Aquitaine, substantial independence from lay power, which allowed it, among other things, to have no interference in the appointment of abbots. The monks of the Cluniac congregation were required to pursue an exclusively spiritual life, according to a strict observance of the Benedictine rule, turning away from earthly goods.

Thanks to certain of its leading personalities, such as Oddone or Maiolo, the so-called Cluniac reform expanded throughout Europe with the foundation of monasteries adhering to the new ideas or with the reform of some already existing ones.

Alongside the monastic reform movement, other feeble attempts at change in secular society also began, although these efforts were initially isolated and without continuity. The situation changed with the accession to the German throne of Henry III of Franconia, known as the Black, considered one of the greatest German emperors. With him a theocratic empire took shape where the ruler represented the leadership of both temporal and religious society, as he was considered chosen and anointed by God and thus his direct representative on Earth.

Fully recognizing the sacred function of his role, Henry III surrounded himself with advisers belonging to the ecclesiastical world and great promoters of the reform born in the monasteries, such as Odilon of Cluny, Richard of Saint-Vanne, and Brunon of Toul, the future Pope Leo IX. It was also thanks to this circle of reformers that Henry proved to be very sensitive to the themes of the movement and in particular was influenced by the Cluniac spirit, no doubt also because of his second marriage to

Agnes of Poitou originally from the House of Acquitania who founded with William I the monastery of Cluny.

However, despite Henry's adherence to the reformation and some concessions he made regarding the independence of monasteries, he did not entirely renounce his prerogative to invest bishops and abbots of his choice with a lot of pastoral staff and the episcopal ring; in fact, this custom continued to be practiced throughout his reign without arousing particular opposition, at least in the secular church, while in monastic circles some criticism began to be raised about the traditional oath of allegiance to the emperor to which abbots were obliged. This power of investiture proved to be one of the cornerstones of the emperor's policy; in fact, once he had consolidated his power in Germany, he looked to Italy, where, in order to strengthen his authority, he proceeded to appoint a large number of German clergymen loyal to him to head dioceses scattered throughout the peninsula.

In 1046 Henry descended to Italy to attend the Council of Sutri with the aim of bringing order to a crisis in the papacy, at the center of which was the clash of three pontiffs who considered themselves legitimate: Benedict IX supported by the Counts of Tusculum, Sylvester III of the Crescenzi family, and Gregory VI who had purchased the papacy from the former. Benedict IX was deposed,

Sylvester III considered a usurper, and Gregory VI had to renounce the office and was later sent into exile and excommunicated as he was accused of simony. The ruler also had Suidger, bishop of Bamberg, elected as the new pope, who took the name Clement II and on the following Christmas crowned Henry himself as emperor of the Holy Roman Empire.

Henry's intervention at Sutri found much support within the church reform movement itself, but opposing voices were also raised, such as that of Bishop Wazone of Liege, who believed that it was not the sovereign's right to depose a pope, even if he was simoniacal. In any case, in addition to being emperor, Henry had also had himself appointed Roman patrician, a position that allowed him to directly influence future elections of the Roman pontiff. In fact, the later Damasus II, Leo IX, and Victor II were all Germans, thus outsiders to Roman circles, and trusted by the emperor, helping to import the model of the imperial church to Rome. With them, the reform finally left the monastic environment and spilled over into the secular church.

In particular, it was the pontificate of Leo IX that saw an acceleration of the reform process, as he was surrounded by a group of valuable collaborators who went on to form the college of cardinals, to whom he entrusted important positions, including: Alinardo, Umberto di Silva Candida,

Federico Gozzelon, future Stephen IX, Ildebrando di Soana former secretary of Gregory VI and future Gregory VII. These theologians played a decisive role in providing doctrinal justifications for a strengthening of the papacy that was to be given the exclusive power to appoint and depose high ecclesiastical offices.

The crisis of the empire during the minority age of Henry IV

On April 19, 1054, Leo IX died in Rome and was succeeded by Gebehard of Eichstatt as Victor II, who was strongly committed to the still purely moral reform. His action was, however, conditioned by the death of Emperor Henry III (Oct. 5, 1056), who left his wife Agnes of Poitou as regent and his young son (the future Henry IV) still a minor.

Agnes immediately proved to be an insecure ruler and weakened the imperial figure. Thus, upon the death of Victor II on June 23, 1057 from malaria, the series of German popes ended, placing the Church in need of finding support outside the Empire. This was found in the margrave of Tuscany and duke of Lorraine Goffredo il Barbuto who, in return for his service, had his brother, Frederick of Lorraine, elected by the cardinals as Stephen IX: this was the first papal election since 1046 that took place without the interference of the Emperor.

Stephen IX's pontificate did not last long and was not particularly decisive; the Lorraine pope, in fact, died as early as 1058 and was succeeded on January 24, 1059, by Nicholas II, born Gerard of Florence, who, with the military support of Goffredo il Barbuto, excommunicated the previously elected antipope Benedict X from the powerful Roman Tuscolani family and was enthroned on January 24, 1059.

With Nicholas II a new phase in the reform of the ecclesiastical structure took shape: in fact, he initiated not only a moral reform but also an institutional one, following the advice of Umberto di Silva Candida, according to whom it would never be possible to reform the Church until the power of episcopal investiture was brought exclusively into the hands of the pope. Nicholas II, therefore, not only struck down the abuses of simony and the marriage of priests, but identified the causes, the roots, of these abuses precisely in the granting by the laity of the investiture of major ecclesiastical offices. He, therefore, claimed the "freedom of the Church" and the exclusive right to confer offices, freeing himself from the customary legal power of the laity: thus the so-called "struggle for investitures" began to emerge.

In September 1059 Nicholas II convened a Roman synod at which the papal bull *In nomine Domini* (also known as *Decretum in electione papae*) was promulgated, with the collaboration of Umberto di Silva Candida, Ildebrando di Soana and Pier Damiani, which, by validating his own inauguration to the Roman see, imposed the procedure to be followed for the election of his successors. This severed the pope's choice from any connection (other than merely formal, such as the applause of confirmation) with the Roman people and the emperor himself. In little more than a decade, then, the system of papal election changed radically: in 1046, Henry III, having deposed all contenders for the papacy, had placed the election effectively under the decision of the emperor, removing it from the control of the Roman noble families and from the clergy of Rome itself; in 1059, on the other hand, the appointment was removed not only from the Roman nobility but also from the authority of the emperor, although the emperor continued to be considered the ruler of Rome and of the whole world.

Nicholas II realized the revolutionary significance of his decision and sought to secure a political-military force capable of enforcing it; so he found a valuable ally in the Norman people: setting out for southern Italy in September 1059, he entered into the Treaty of Melfi with Robert Guiscard and Richard I of Aversa, according to which, in a typically feudal logic, the Normans paid homage of submission and an oath of allegiance to the pope, recognizing themselves as his subjects, while the Roman Church, in the figure of the pontiff, granted them investiture over all the territories they conquered. In this way they were no longer considered foreign invaders of the peninsula, but received the right to rule, promising to lend faithful military aid to the pontiff. With a single move Nicholas II had won feudal sovereignty over much of Italy but, at the same time, violated the imperial right of Henry IV, with whom tense and difficult relations began.

With the death of Nicholas II, the group of reforming cardinals proceeded to elect Anselm of Lucca, a native of Milan, who was installed in 1061 under the name of Alexander II in the manner expressed in the *Decretum in electione papae* issued by his predecessor and therefore without the Empress Agnes being involved. Shortly thereafter, in 1062, in order to re-establish the authority of the Empire undermined by the weakness shown by Agnes, the German princes, led by the Archbishop of Cologne Annon, kidnapped the crown prince, still a minor, taking him to Cologne and formally entrusting him with imperial power under the name of Henry IV ("coup d'état" of Kaiserswerth).

In the meantime, with the pontificate of Alexander II the idea of a strengthening of the theory of papal primacy began to spread more and more, especially with regard to the pontiff's exclusive prerogative in calling councils and investing the highest ecclesiastical offices; a thesis already long since reiterated by theologians such as Wazone of

Liege first, Pier Damiani and Sigrfrido of Gorze later. Such new ideas would in a short time lead the Church to clash against the Empire, as soon as the latter returned to authority with the coming of age of Emperor Henry IV, in a conflict that would go down in history as the "struggle for investitures," which would see Hildebrand of Soana, successor to Pope Alexander II, who died on April 21, 1073, as the absolute protagonist.

The struggle begins: the clash between Henry IV and Gregory VII

The election of Hildebrand of Soana and the *Dictatus Papae*

During the funeral of Alexander II on April 22, 1073, the assembled crowd began to loudly acclaim Hildebrand of Soana as the new pope; on the same day, he was taken to St. Peter in Chains to be legally elected by the cardinals present to the papal dignity, with the pontifical name of Gregory VII. This procedure, however, did not fail to arouse contestation, since it did not fully conform to the provisions of the *Decretum in electione papae.* In the future, Hildebrando's opponents, particularly Guibert of Ravenna (future antipope), would often refer to this to delegitimize his authority.

From the outset, Gregory put in place his policy of protecting the independence of the church from secular power, engaging in negotiations favored by the support also coming from some of the bishops of the Empire. The goal was to "impose on the church an organizational model of a monarchical nature and on the desacralization of the imperial office." As for relations with the Holy Roman Empire, the pope was in a favorable situation; the weakness of the German monarchy resulting from the death of Henry III had been exacerbated by the rebellion of the Saxons that his son Henry IV, much younger than the pontiff, was facing.

In 1074, Gregory decided to settle a matter of canon law with King Henry immediately before his coronation as emperor could take place: five of his councillors stood excommunicated but continued to be present at his court. At first, Henry submitted to the pope: he dissolved his relations with them, made an act of penance at Nuremberg in the presence of the papal legates, and swore an oath of obedience to the pope, promising support for church reform. Henry's conciliatory attitude, which had earned him the pontiff's confidence, changed rapidly as soon as he succeeded in defeating the Saxons at the Langensalza battle, fought on June 9, 1075. Invigorated by the victory, Henry changed policy, aiming to reassert his power as king of the Romans and king of Italy. In September of that year, following the murder of the Milanese pataria exponent Erlembaldo Cotta, he invested the cleric Tedaldo, archbishop of Milan, as well as the bishops of the dioceses of Fermo and Spoleto, thus failing in his commitments. This action, in open contrast to Pope Gregory, is regarded as the spark that set off the "investiture struggle." However, in addition to the issue concerning investitures, the fate of the *dominium mundi*, the clash between priestly power and imperial power, referred to by 12th-century historians as "Discidium inter sacerdotium et regnum," was at stake.

1075 was, probably, also the year in which Gregory VII drafted the famous *Dictatus Papae* ("*Principled Statements of the Pope*"), a collection of uncertain nature of twenty-seven propositions, each of which enunciates a specific power of the Roman pontiff. The document expresses Gregory VII's theocratic vision: the superiority of the pontifical institution over all secular rulers, including the emperor, is unquestioned, thus counteracting caesaropapism, i.e., the interference of political power in the government of the Church. The pope derives his authority from God "by the grace of the prince of the apostles" (St. Peter), and it is by virtue of this grace that the pope exercises the power to bind and to dissolve. From the *Dictatus* the relationship between state and church emerged completely turned upside down: it was no longer the emperor who approved the pope's appointment, but it was the pope who gave the emperor his power and, eventually, revoked it. There is no doubt that such a view was intended to recover the doctrine of the two powers proposed by Pope Gelasius I in the fifth century, according to which all of Christendom, ecclesiastical and secular, was to be subject to the moral magistracy of the Roman Pontiff; for Gregory "the apostolic dignity was the sun, the royal dignity the moon."

The accusations against Gregory in the synod of Worms

Throughout 1075 Henry IV continued to impart investitures of German bishops, although he no longer accepted monetary offers. As mentioned, the clash between the two institutions arose from the appointment of the archbishop of Milan, a very important seat for church-empire relations: as the Lombard city was traditionally close to the emperor, the archbishop often played a mediating role between pope and king of the Romans. In 1074 both Gregory VII and Henry IV had approved the appointment of Attone, an ecclesiastic close to the Patarines, and the following year, taking advantage of the weakness of the Patarines, the ruler preferred Tedaldo of Castiglione.He intervened in other ecclesiastical matters pertinent to Italy: he sent Count Eberard to Lombardy to fight the Patarines (supported instead by the Church of Rome) and openly supported the archbishop of Ravenna Guiberto in opposition to the Roman pontiff. Finally, he sought an alliance with the Norman Duke Robert of Altavilla. Gregory VII protested in a harsh letter, dated December 8, 1075, accusing Henry of continuing to listen to the five excommunicated councillors.; he then demanded that he acknowledge his sins and repent of them, however, showing himself willing to amend with him the text of the decree against lay investitures.

In late 1075 Gregory VII suffered an attack, from which Henry IV inferred that the pontiff no longer had the favor of the Romans. Moreover, he knew that the powerful Robert of Altavilla, who had been excommunicated, would not intervene in defense of the pope in the event of an attack on Rome. He then thought of striking the decisive blow by convening a council of the bishops of Germany in Worms, which met on January 24, 1076.

Among the senior German clerics were many enemies of the pontiff, including a cardinal, Hugh of Remiremont called Candide, once an ally but now his adversary. Hugh traveled to Germany for the occasion and before the council made a series of accusations against the pope that were favorably received. In a document filled with other charges against him, the German bishops declared that they no longer accepted obedience to Gregory VII and no longer recognized him as pope.

In a letter, Henry made him aware of the deposition ruling to which he declared his adherence and invited him to resign:

The ruling referred to a passage from St. Paul's letter to the Galatians, "If anyone preaches to you a gospel other than the one you have received, let him be anathema!" thus insinuating that Gregory could even be equated with false prophets. The council sent two bishops to Italy who obtained an act of deposition from the Lombard bishops gathered at a synod in Piacenza. The German bishops justified Gregory's deposition by claiming the alleged irregularity of his election, which took place by popular acclamation and not according to the canons. It was also claimed that he had previously sworn that he would never accept the papal office and that he intimately consorted with some women.

Henry's excommunication

Gregory's response was not long in coming; the following day the pope disclaimed the schismatic councils of Worms and Piacenza and excommunicated Archbishop Siegfried I of Mainz as president of the assembly. Vindicating the legitimacy of his pontificate, he also pronounced a sentence of excommunication against Henry IV by stripping him of his royal dignity and dissolving his subjects from the oath of allegiance sworn in his favor. For the first time a pope not only excommunicated a ruler, but inhibited him from exercising his royal power. Unlike Henry, however, Gregory did not formally sanction the monarch's deposition, but rather considered him suspended until he repented. What this effect actually produced, or whether it remained a vain threat, depended not so much on Gregory as on Henry's subjects and, above all, on the German princes; documents of the time suggest that the king's excommunication created a deep impression and division among Christians, as they had become accustomed to a theocratic and sacred conception of the ruler.

The decree of excommunication reached Henry in Utrecht on Easter Eve (March 26); his reaction was immediate: on that same day he responded with a very harsh letter, in which he called Gregory "not pope, but a false monk," declared him deposed and, addressing the Romans in his capacity as a patrician, asked them to abandon him and elect a new pope.

Thirty years earlier, Henry III had deposed three popes who had tried to usurp the throne of Peter, as mentioned, and Henry IV had imitated this procedure, but without matching its success; indeed, Gregory's ruling produced a resounding effect in Germany: there was, among the German bishops, a rapid and general change of sentiment in favor of the pontiff. Secular princes seized the opportunity to pursue their anti-regal policies under the aura of respectability provided by the papal decision. When, on Pentecost Day (May 15), the king proposed to discuss measures to be taken against Gregory at a council with his nobles, only a few showed up. A second convocation in Mainz for the feast of St. Peter (June 15) went deserted. The Saxons took advantage of this to rise up, and the anti-Royalist party increased its strength more and more. Only Lombardy remained loyal to Henry.

The humiliation of Canossa

As a result of the excommunication, many German princes previously supporters of the emperor turned their backs on him; on October 16 a diet of princes and bishops met in Trebur, a town on the Rhine in Hesse, to examine the king's position, which was also attended by the papal legate Altmann of Passau. The princes declared that Henry should ask the pope's pardon and pledge obedience; they also decided that if within a year and a day of his excommunication (i.e., by Feb. 2 of the following year) the condemnation still remained in force, the throne would be considered vacant. Concerned, Henry IV saw fit to negotiate: he issued a written promise to obey the Holy See and comply with its wishes. The princes agreed that a general diet of the kingdom, presided over by the pontiff himself, would be held in February 1077 in Augsburg, Bavaria. On that occasion the final sentence on Henry would be pronounced.

Gregory VII ratified the agreement and planned to travel to Germany. The situation had at that time become extremely critical for Henry, for whom it was imperative, under any circumstances and at any price, to secure Gregory's absolution before the expiration of the year, otherwise it would have been almost impossible to prevent his opponents from attacking him by justifying himself with excommunication. He therefore decided to go to Hildebrus and set out in December crossing the snowy Alps. Because his adversaries, Rudolph of Swabia and Berthold I of Zähringen, prevented him from accessing German passes, the emperor was forced to cross the Mont Cenis Pass.

In the meantime, the pope had already departed from Rome, and on January 8, 1077, he arrived in Mantua, in the possessions of Countess Matilda, whom he was to accompany from there as far as the Verona Locks, where he would find the escort of the German princes who would lead him as far as Augsburg. But, because of the great frost that year, the crossing of the Alps proved prohibitive. News reached Gregory that Henry was on his way to meet him, accompanied by his wife Bertha and their son Conrad, still an infant. The king, who had traveled through Burgundy, was enthusiastically welcomed by the Lombards, who also provided him with an armed escort. The pontiff, lacking armed support, did not feel safe in Lombardy, so he decided to retreat and, retracing his steps, stopped at Canossa, in the Reggio Emilia region, as a guest of Matilda.

Thanks to the intercession of the countess and Henry's godfather Hugh of Cluny, Gregory agreed to meet the emperor on January 25, 1077, the feast of the conversion of St. Paul. Chronicles tell that Henry had appeared before the castle of Canossa, in the Apennines of Reggio, in penitent dress, and after three days the pontiff lifted his excommunication, only five days before the deadline set by the opposing princes. The image of Henry going to Canossa in an attitude of humble penitence is essentially based on one main source, Lambert of Hersfeld, a strong supporter of the pope and a member of the opposition nobility. The penance was, in any case, a formal act, performed by Henry, and one that the pope could not refuse; it appears today as a clever diplomatic maneuver, which provided the emperor with freedom of action while limiting that of the pope. However, it is certain that, in the long run, this event dealt a severe blow to the authority of the German Empire.

Henry's gesture became a historic event of great resonance, although it did not change the course of events: the absolution from excommunication was the outcome of prolonged negotiations and occurred only upon the king's assumption of precise commitments. Gregory VII asserted supreme papal authority over kings, vesting in them the authority to establish the conditions under which they could exercise royal power and under which their subjects were required to obey them. With the submission of Canossa Henry IV recognized this papal privilege. It was with reluctance that the pope accepted the repentance since in this way the diet of princes at Augsburg, in which he had reasonable hopes of acting as arbiter, would have become useless or, if it had succeeded in convening, would have changed his character completely. It was, however, impossible to deny the penitent a return to the Church, and Gregory's religious obligations overrode political interests.

The removal of the condemnation did not, however, imply true reconciliation, and there was no basis for the resolution of the great issue at stake: that of investiture. A new conflict was therefore inevitable for the simple fact that Henry IV, of course, considered the sentence of deposition annulled along with that of excommunication;

while Gregory, for his part, was intent on reserving his freedom of action.

The anti-King and the Emperor's second excommunication

While Henry IV was still in Italy and negotiating his absolution from excommunication, the German nobles who opposed him ganged up against him. Not only did they persist in their policy even after his absolution, but they were determined in installing, on March 15, 1077, at Forchheim, a rival king in the person of Duke Rudolf of Swabia; the princes who elevated him to the throne made him promise never to resort to simoniacal practices in the allocation of episcopal offices.

Moreover, he was obliged to grant princes the right to vote in the imperial election and was denied the right to transfer his title to any sons, negating the hitherto prevailing dynastic principle; the latter represented the first step toward the free election demanded by the princes of the Empire. The papal legates present at the election were apparently neutral, and Gregory himself tried to maintain this attitude in the following years; his task was made easier as the two parties were of equal strength, each seeking a decisive advantage that would bring the pope to his side. Nevertheless, the result of this neutrality was that he lost much of the trust of both parties.

In June, Henry excluded Rudolf from the Empire and began to confront him in what is commonly known as the Great Saxon Revolt. He suffered two initial defeats: on August 7, 1078 at the Battle of Mellrichstadt and on January 27, 1080 at the Battle of Flarchheim. After the latter defeat, Gregory chose to side with the victor, the anti-king Rudolf, thus abandoning, under pressure from the Saxons, the wait-and-see policy and pronouncing, on March 7, again for the deposition and excommunication of King Henry.

The second papal condemnation did not have the same consequences as the previous one: the sovereign, more experienced at a distance of four years, faced the confrontation with the pontiff with great vigor and refused to recognize the condemnation, claiming its illegality. He therefore convened a council of the Germanic episcopate in Brixen, where the protagonist was again Hugh Candide, who accused the pontiff of being a murderer and a heretic. On June 26, 1080, Henry IV declared Gregory deposed and appointed Archbishop Guibert of Ravenna as his successor. In addition, at the battle on the Elster the following October 14, Rudolph, despite having captured a victory, lost his right hand and was shot dead in the abdomen, dying the following day. The loss of his right hand, the hand of the oath of allegiance made to Henry at the beginning of his reign, was used politically by his supporters (describing it as a judgment from God) to further weaken the opposition nobility.

In the meantime, the pontiff met with the Norman dukes Robert of Altavilla and Robert Guiscard at Ceprano (a town located about halfway between Rome and Naples, on the Via Casilina) where they made a treaty. On June 29, 1080, he withdrew his excommunication and handed back the title of duke, along with the conquered territories. The Holy See definitively renounced the former territories of the Byzantine Empire in southern Italy, but felt it had acquired a loyal ally. The act was essentially a reconfirmation of the investiture conferred on the two dukes by their predecessor popes, who saw in the Normans a possible useful military aid to protect the reformation. In fact, they became vassals of the papacy, were required to pay a not-so-symbolic census payment and, above all, pledged to help the Church to "maintain, acquire and defend the *regalia of* St. Peter and its possessions [...] to securely and honorably maintain the Roman papacy."

The emperor in Italy and the sack of Rome

In 1081 Henry, on the strength of the victory he had achieved the previous year over Rudolphus, opened the conflict against Gregory in Italy. He then crossed the Alps and in February 1082 reached the gates of Rome, where he held negotiations, which were, however, rejected. He then put his hand to force and attempted to set fire to the Vatican basilica. With the new year, 1083, he returned to camp under the walls of Rome. After seven months of siege, the city had weakened and Henry was able to cross the walls of the Lion City, forcing Gregory VII to take refuge in Castel Sant'Angelo. The king remained in the city until late autumn; he then returned home confident that he had Rome in his hands. Subsequently, Gregory convened a synod of bishops for November 20. The council did not explicitly excommunicate Henry, but rather "all those" who had prevented bishops close to the Holy See from taking part.

Learning of this, Henry re-entered Rome on March 21, 1084. The whole city was in his hands except Castel Sant'Angelo, where Pope Gregory, whom by now most of the cardinals had turned their backs, continued to resist. This was followed by the convocation of a council in St. Peter's on March 24 to judge the pope, who was excommunicated and deposed; in his place was installed in St. John Lateran Guibert of Ravenna, who took the name Clement III. On March 31 Clement crowned Henry IV as emperor.

After several months of siege and fruitless negotiations, Gregory VII sent for the Norman Robert of Altavilla, duke of Apulia and Calabria, to come to his rescue. Hearing the news, the antipope Clement III and Henry IV departed

Rome on May 21. Three days later Norman troops entered Rome and freed the pontiff. The Duke of Altavilla's soldiers devastated the Urbe making themselves responsible for worse looting and destruction, when compared to those of the Gothic sack of 410 and the Lansquenet sack of 1527. Much of the ancient remains then still standing, as well as the churches, were stripped and destroyed; from then on the whole population of Rome was concentrated in the Campus Martius (the bend of the Tiber) and the whole sector corresponding to Aventine, Esquiline, Caelian remained uninhabited for centuries. Hugh of Flavigny, recounting the events, spoke of great misdeeds, rape and violence, carried out against the guilty and the innocent.

The catastrophe that had befallen the Eternal City was the final blow that sank the bond between Gregory VII and Rome. In the eyes of the Romans he represented nothing more than the man who had brought a series of misfortunes upon the city. Gregory understood that when the Norman troops returned to their territories, the Romans would plot their revenge against him. He therefore decided, in June 1083, to leave Rome in the wake of the Hauteville troops and repair to the Mezzogiorno. Rome had been left undefended: it was easy for Clement III to regain possession of the city.

With the arrival in Rome of the antipope Clement III, the situation had become very confusing: some German bishops were reluctant to support the election of an antipope, while most of those at the head of dioceses in northern Italy were suspended by Gregory VII in 1085. In response, Henry IV had deposed all Germanic bishops who supported the exiled pope.

Gregory VII spent the last years of his life in Salerno, a city that was part of the domains of Robert of Hauteville. He consecrated the cathedral and toward the end of the year convened his last council in which he renewed the excommunication against Henry IV and Clement III. On May 25, 1085, he died.

The struggle for investiture in France and England.

In France

The situation in France was profoundly different from that evident in Germany or England: the power of the Capetian dynasty, on the throne unchallenged since 987, was actually exercised over a territory that was still very modest compared to that of later centuries, comprising only a few dioceses and over some of which the influence was in any case modest; the remaining regions were in fact under the control of the nobility.

With the Council of Rheims in 1049, Pope Leo IX intervened profoundly in the French church, where he could not count on a reform-sensitive ruler, as was the case in the Empire of Henry III: in France, it was more important for Henry I to rely on bishops of proven political reliability than religious qualities, as he needed their economic and military input so that he could maintain feudal supremacy over his vassals.

The popes, therefore, had to take personal action so that the high ecclesiastical offices of France could be assigned according to the canons and so that the frequent situations of simony and marriage in the clergy could be eradicated. To achieve these ends the pontiffs resorted to the action of legates who were given the task of spreading the decrees and upholding their observance. Despite the inevitable clashes between these reformers and the sovereigns, a serious conflict was never reached, preferring to opt for agreements and compromises.

The situation became more tense when Gregory VII appointed two French bishops as his permanent representatives: Hugh of Die, for Burgundy and the northern regions, and Amatus of Oleron for the more southern regions. Of the two it was Hugh who acted most decisively by removing several bishops who were considered simoniacs, and at the same time in the synod of Autun the prohibition of the temporal power to intervene in ecclesiastical appointments was declared. The bishop's action faced hostility from much of the episcopate of France, which vigorously rejected having to submit to him. King Philip I of France, on the other hand, maintained a moderate profile while continuing to show little interest in the spread of reform.

In England

In 1066 the Norman Duke William the Conqueror, having obtained permission from Pope Gregory VII despite opposition from the curia, invaded England, wresting it from the Anglo-Saxons. Having completed his conquest of the island, he vigorously imposed church reform on his new territories, partly through the action of Lanfranc of Pavia, who was appointed archbishop of Canterbury in 1070. William had the English Church routed toward a feudal-type model in which bishops and abbots were obliged to provide, in the same way as the barons of the realm, a quota of armed men for the needs of the crown. Despite this, the strong control exercised by the duke over the church eventually cooled relations with Gregory VII, aided by William's refusal to take the feudal oath to the church. Moreover, the English crown enjoyed enough power to remain neutral in the complicated struggle between the pontiff and Emperor Henry IV. The situation remained unchanged with William's successor, his son William II the Red.

Things changed with the appointment as archbishop of Canterbury of Anselm of Aosta who, strongly attached to his obligations to the Church, fought for reform and against simony by refusing to be considered a feudal lord of the English crown. His initiative led him into a bitter clash with King William II that ended in his exile from which he could return only on the king's death, when his successor Henry I, of sincere religious faith and in need of all support as a cadet and not initially destined for the throne, took the throne. The latter solemnly promised to respect the freedoms of the Church but did not go so far as to accept the ban on investiture by the laity and feudal oath taking by clerics that Anselm demanded of him as a result of what had transpired at the Council of Rome held in early 1099. Despite this opposition, Anselm and Henry sought a compromise solution moved by "Anselm out of a spontaneous desire for peace, the king out of political considerations, and the curia because it did not want to jeopardize England's obedience and union with Rome."

Despite the agreement signed in 1107, the dominance of the English crown over the Church remained unchanged suffering, however, a decline during the dispute (known as "anarchy") between Stephen of Blois and Matilda over the crown that favored the influence of Rome. The murder of Thomas Becket in 1170 during the reign of Henry II of England halted the English Church's independence turn.

An ideological struggle

The struggle that pitted Church reformers and the Empire against each other had not only military implications but was also an ideological conflict made up of writings, sermons, and rallies in the squares that came to involve, perhaps for the first time in a long time, the ideals of the popular masses. Between 1080 and 1085, 24 mutually contradictory formulations were drafted by both sides of the conflict and, in all, some 150 Latin texts on the subject of the investiture struggle circulated. The violent denunciations forwarded by Henry IV's chancery had been answered by the lengthy letters Gregory VII sent to clerics, some of which forbade receiving the sacraments from a married or unchaste priest, while others threatened to deprive the faithful of the sacraments. The ban on simony also provoked numerous debates about the legitimacy of temporal power within the Church and the proposal to exclude from the clergy all those who had received investiture from an antipope or supporter of the emperor. The two most prominent theologians of the time who addressed the issue were Pier Damiani and Umberto di Silva Candida, the latter of clearly more intransigent positions than the former.

In a society where the clergy were the main repositories of knowledge and the ability to write, the pope could count on a large number of ecclesiastical authors. The monasteries loyal to the pontiff's theses were an effective intermediary, and Manegold of Lautenbach even went so far as to theorize that royal authority was a delegation of power by the people, who could withdraw it if the monarch behaved like a tyrant and did not act in the interests of the people. The imperial party, on the other hand, advocated the theses of the divine institution of kingship and the sacredness of the mission of the emperor, head and protector of the Christian people. The jurists of Bologna and Padua proposed a new interpretation of Roman law, whereby the emperor was confirmed as sovereign and the pope as merely a subject like all others. Sigebert of Gembloux put the debate in a historical perspective: the Empire had passed from the Romans to the Franks and from the Franks to the Germans, therefore, sooner or later, all kingdoms would join the Empire, as this was God's will.

The continuation with the successors of Gregory

The death of Henry IV

Upon Gregory VII's death, no pope was elected for two years; the sede vacante ended with the election of the frail Victor III, whose pontificate lasted only ten months. This sudden weakness of the papacy led Henry IV to believe that a decisive victory would be within his grasp, however unfinished the difficulties were for him. Victor III was succeeded by Urban II, a Cluniac monk of a decidedly different temperament and ready to oppose the emperor, who in the meantime was busy dealing with two revolts: the first one broke out in Bavaria in 1086 and a second one led by his son Conrad of Lorraine, elected king of Germany in 1087, but instigated by Countess Matilda of Canossa. Between 1093 and 1097 Conrad, by occupying the passes of the Alps, succeeded in depriving his father stranded in Italy of any chance of returning to Germany. At the same time, Urban II had embarked on a journey to France where he attended the Council of Clermont in 1095; on that occasion he made the famous appeal to

Christendom from which sprang the first crusade by which all of Western Christian society was mobilized. In 1099 he died and the papal throne went to Paschal II, also a Cluniac monk.

In 1105 Paschal II supported a conspiracy hatched against Emperor Henry IV and organized by Empress Adelaide of Kiev and her second son, the future Henry V. The latter, after having his brother Conrad deposed five years earlier, had managed to take command of the German nobility. The conspiracy was successful, and Henry IV, taken prisoner, was forced to abdicate in favor of his son at the imperial diet of Mainz. Henry IV would die in 1106 in Liege, still excommunicated and unable to receive a religious burial until 1111, when he would be interred in Speyer Cathedral. In the meantime, the Germanic Church, weary of the conflict, had become convinced of the negative effects produced by simony, and so the bishops had begun to abandon political affairs to devote themselves more and more to the religious aspects proper to their ministry. Despite Henry IV's stubborn resistance throughout his life, the Gregorian reform had now spread throughout Germany.

The conflict between Henry V and Paschal

Although Henry V initially leaned on supporters of the Gregorian reform to depose his father, as soon as he had consolidated his power he changed his attitude, opposing papal power and resuming the custom of investing bishops. For his part, Paschal II, after renewing the prohibition for the secular power to persevere with this practice, thought he could negotiate by taking advantage of the fact that Henry V himself wished to be crowned emperor by the pope. When he traveled to Italy in the hope of being able to persuade Paschal II, the latter proposed to him a radical solution aimed at permanently severing the ties between episcopacy and empire. The ruler, unable to accede to such a radical demand, renounced secular investitures but in return obtained that the bishops surrender the *insignia*, that is, the rights over cities, duchies, marquisates, tolls, and currencies over markets that they held on the basis of their administrative functions. These concessions aroused strong opposition from the Roman Curia and the Germanic bishops.

On February 12, 1111, during the coronation ceremony, before the bishops made their protests explicit, Henry V declared the agreement unenforceable, prompting the pontiff's refusal to proceed further with the rite. Paschal was then imprisoned and, three months later, forced to sign what sources call the "privilege of Ponte Mammolo," by which the emperor was crowned and at the same time given the power of investiture with ring and crosier. The imperial faction thus seemed to triumph, however, the high ecclesiastical levels could not accept this situation and so the Lateran Council of 1112 declared null and void all concessions made during the papal imprisonment. Moreover, the king was faced with general discontent rampant throughout Germany, and it was there in his reign that imperial troops suffered two serious defeats. In 1114 he was excommunicated and, this time, the German clergy sided with the pope and two reforming bishops were appointed in Metz and Magdeburg. Nevertheless, Henry V incorporated the Italian fiefdoms belonging to Matilda of Canossa into the Empire's dominions in 1115. Paschal II died in 1118 and the new pontiff, Gelasius II, refused to meet the emperor for fear of imprisonment and left Rome when the latter arrived. As before his father, the ruler elected an antipope, Gregory VIII.

Peace: the Concordat of Worms

Gelasius II died in exile in Cluny in January 1119. The Germanic prelates, tired of the conflict, hoped for a solution that would satisfy both sides. The new pope, Callistus II, immediately began negotiations with the emperor, in which papal legates William of Champeaux, Peter Abelard and Pontius of Melgueil participated, but without achieving the hoped-for success. While the imperial army and the rebels of Saxony were ready to clash, the Germanic princes, assembled at the initiative of the archbishop of Trier, ordered Henry V to submit to the pope if he preserved "the honor of the Empire." Thus began a year of difficult negotiations that led to several excommunications, including those of the antipope Gregory VIII, many supporters of the empire, such as the Bolognese jurist Irnerius, and that of the sovereign himself. It was the papal legate Lamberto da Bologna, bishop of Ostia and future Honorius II, who carried out the diplomatic activity necessary to mend the rift. Thus, thanks to him, after obtaining papal pardon, the emperor's excommunication was withdrawn without his being required to do penance.

However, the final compromise was reached on September 23, 1122 through the well-known concordat of Worms, a model for later developments in church-empire relations. According to the concordat, the emperor renounced his prerogative of investiture with staff and pastoral ring by accepting the free election of bishops by the chapter of cathedral canons. However, he or his representative was guaranteed the opportunity to attend the appointment and, if conflicts arose, to intervene in favor of the candidate he considered most worthy. In addition, again the sovereign was allowed to enact the temporal investiture of the bishop in the form of the handing over of a scepter, a symbol that had no spiritual connotation but represented the transfer of undefined *regalia* that corresponded to certain legal duties. This in Germany had to take place before spiritual investiture, while in Italy and Burgundy only after ordination had taken place, a sign that in that territory the influence of the empire in the appointment of bishops and abbots had now waned. Finally, papacy and empire signed a promise to preserve the peace they had reached. The agreement, then, seemed to end the struggle over investitures and marked the beginning of the decline of caesaropapism in the West.

The papacy succeeded, for a time, in wresting control of the secular clergy from the monarchs, thus strengthening its prestige; Callistus II hastened to convene an ecumenical council (Lateran Council I), the first since the Council of Constantinople in 869, by which the provisions of the Worms Concordat were ratified, simony, marriage or concubinage of the clergy was again condemned, and a clampdown was placed on the influence of the laity over the property and income of the Church. The papacy acquired the elements and characteristics of a monarchy, but the Holy See still failed to impose its *dominium mundi*. The separation of temporal and spiritual power allowed for a gradual secularization of imperial power, which gradually weakened. Indeed, excommunications and depositions began to undermine the structures of feudal society. The compromise largely resulted in a defeat for the empire: prelates were no longer the officers of the temporal ruler, but vassals, like secular princes, and the administrative structure of the Ottonians lost its solidity.

Despite reaching this compromise, the conflict was still not completely over. It resumed vigor in 1154 with the beginning of the so-called "dispute between priesthood and empire" that ended, a century later, with the total defeat of the Germanic emperors. Around 1220, Frederick II of Swabia even ended up renouncing the privileges he had been granted by the Worms concordat on Germanic soil.

The Dictatus Papae

It is believed that in 1075 Gregory VII wrote the famous *Dictatus Papae* ("Principle Statements of the Pope"), a collection of twenty-seven numbered propositions, perhaps a programmatic document or an index of a larger work that was never completed, each of which enunciates a specific power or right of the Roman pontiff. In fact, the exact date of this work is not certain, the traditional placement in 1075 stems from the fact that it was sandwiched between two missives dated in March of that year, but while there is no certainty about this, there is also no reason to believe that this dating is incorrect. This controversial document expresses Gregory VII's theocratic vision: the superiority of the papal institution over all secular rulers, including the emperor, is unquestioned, thus counteracting caesaropapism, that is, the interference of political power in the government of the Church. According to this dictate, the authority of the pontiff derives directly from God "by the grace of the prince of the apostles" (St. Peter), and it is by virtue of this grace that the pope exercises absolute power to bind and to dissolve.

According to what emerges from the *Dictatus*, the relationship between state and church was to be completely reversed from the *status quo*: it was no longer the emperor who approved the pope's appointment, but it was the pope who had the right to grant the emperor his power and, eventually, to revoke it. Again according to the statements made, obedience to the Church must be absolute; anyone who did not comply was practically considered a heretic and therefore liable to excommunication. Some historians have pointed out that the spirit of this legislation is an attempt to recover the doctrine of the two powers instituted by Pope Gelasius I in the fifth century, according to which all of Christendom, ecclesiastical and secular, was to be subject to the moral magistracy of the Roman Pontiff; for Gregory "the apostolic dignity was the sun, the royal dignity the moon." The *Dictatus papae, whatever* its nature (programmatic document or index of a larger work), well summarized the features of the process already under way, accelerated by Gregory VII's policy, which tended toward the transformation of the Church into a de facto theocratic monarchy, with strong centralized power, at the expense of the independence of the dioceses.

In 1076, Gregory VII, in his ruling suspending Henry IV's powers as king of the Romans and king of Italy, will apply Articles XII and XXVII of the document.

Synod of Worms and deposition of Gregory

Throughout 1075 Henry IV continued to impart investitures of German bishops, although he no longer accepted monetary offerings. As mentioned, the clash between the two institutions arose from the appointment of the archbishop of Milan, a very important seat for church-empire relations. As the Lombard city was traditionally close to the emperor, the archbishop often played a mediating role between pope and king of the Romans. In 1074 both the pope and Henry IV had approved the appointment of Attone, a cleric close to the pataria. The following year, taking advantage of the weakness of the Patarians, Henry had appointed Tedald of Castiglione. Gregory VII protested in a harsh letter, dated December 8, 1075, accusing Henry of continuing to listen to the five excommunicated councillors.

In late 1075 Gregory VII suffered an attack: while he was celebrating mass in the church *ad nivem*, today's Santa Maria Maggiore, he was kidnapped by a certain Cencio but soon afterwards freed thanks to the help of the faithful. From this Henry IV deduced that the pontiff no longer had the favor of the Romans and was going through a period of weakness. This conviction was reinforced by the certainty that the powerful Robert of Altavilla, who had been excommunicated, would not intervene in defense of the pope in the event of an attack on Rome. The German king planned, therefore, to strike the decisive blow by convening a council of the bishops of Germany in Worms for January 24, 1076. Gregory had many enemies among the German churchmen, among whom was Cardinal Hugh of Remiremont, known as Candide, once on his side but now his opponent. At the council Hugh made a series of accusations against the pope, which were welcomed by the assembly. The concluding statement went on to state that Gregory could not be considered a legitimate pope and that the German bishops no longer accepted a duty of obedience to him. The deposition ruling was made known to him by a letter from Henry in which he was invited to resign:

The ruling referred to a passage in St. Paul's letter to the Galatians, "If anyone preaches to you a gospel other than the one you have received, let him be anathema!" thus insinuating that Gregory could even be equated with false prophets. The council sent two bishops to Italy who obtained an act of deposition from the Lombard bishops gathered at a synod in Piacenza. The German bishops justified Gregory's deposition by claiming the alleged irregularity of his election, which took place by popular acclamation and not according to the canons. It was also claimed that Gregory had previously sworn that he would never accept the papal office and that he intimately consorted with some women, perhaps a reference to his relations with Countess Matilda of Canossa.

Lenten synod of 1076 and the excommunication of Henry IV

A cleric of the church of Parma, Roland, informed the pope of these decisions during the traditional Lenten synod meeting in the Lateran Basilica between February 14 and 20, 1076. Gregory's response was not long in coming, and the following day he disclaimed the schismatic councils of Worms and Piacenza, excommunicating Archbishop Siegfried I of Mainz as president of the former. Vindicating the legitimacy of his pontificate, he pronounced a sentence of excommunication against Henry IV, stripping him of his royal dignity and, at the same time, dissolving his subjects from the oaths of allegiance taken in his favor.

For the first time, a pope not only excommunicated a ruler but inhibited him from exercising his power. Unlike Henry had done, moreover, Gregory did not formally sanction the monarch's deposition, but rather considered him suspended until he repented. Whether this actually took effect or remained a vain threat depended less on Gregory than on Henry's subjects and, above all, the German princes. Documents of the time suggest that the king's excommunication created a deep impression and division among Christians, as they had become accustomed to a theocratic and sacred conception of the king.

The decree reached Henry in Utrecht on Easter Eve, March 26. His reaction was immediate: on that same day he responded to it with a very harsh letter. He called Gregory "not pope, but a false monk," declared him deposed and, addressing the Romans in his capacity as a patrician, asked them to abandon him and elect a new pontiff.

Thirty years earlier, Henry III had deposed three conflicting popes at the Council of Sutri; his son Henry IV had imitated this procedure but was not as successful. On the contrary, Gregory's excommunication produced a resounding effect in Germany: among the German bishops there was a rapid and general change of sentiment in favor of Gregory, while the secular princes seized the opportunity to pursue their anti-regal claims under the aura of respectability provided by the papal decision. When on the Day of Pentecost the king proposed to discuss the measures to be taken against Gregory in a council with his nobles, only a few showed up. A second convocation in Mainz on June 15 went unheard. The Saxons took advantage of this to rise up, and the anti-Royalist party increased its strength all the more. Only Lombardy remained loyal to Henry.

The Canossa meeting

On October 16 a diet of princes and bishops met in Trebur, a town on the Rhine in Hesse, to examine the king's position, which was also attended by the papal legate Altmann of Passau. The princes declared that

Henry should ask the pope's pardon and pledge obedience; they also decided that if within a year and a day of his excommunication (i.e., by Feb. 2 of the following year) the condemnation still remained in force, the throne would be considered vacant. Concerned, Henry IV issued written promises to obey the Holy See and comply with its wishes. The princes agreed that a general diet of the kingdom would be held in February 1077 in Augsburg, Bavaria, presided over by the pontiff himself. On that occasion the final sentence on Henry would be pronounced.

Gregory VII ratified the agreement and planned the trip to Germany. Henry, needing papal absolution, decided to go to meet Hildebrus and set out in December across the snowy Alps. Because his adversaries, Rudolph of Swabia and Berthold I of Zähringen, prevented him from accessing German passes, the emperor was forced to pass through the Mont Cenis Pass.

In the meantime, the pope had already departed from Rome, and on January 8, 1077, he arrived in Mantua, in the possessions of Countess Matilda. From here the countess was supposed to accompany him as far as the Locks of Verona, where he would find the escort of the German princes all the way to Augsburg, but the frost that year slowed his journey. Gregory learned that Henry was on his way to meet him and was enthusiastically welcomed by the Lombards, who also provided him with an armed escort. The pope, however, lacking armed protection, did not feel safe in Lombardy, so he decided to retreat and retrace his steps, stopping at Canossa, in the Reggio Emilia region, a guest of Matilda.

Thanks to the intercession of the countess and Henry's godfather Hugh of Cluny, Gregory agreed to meet the emperor on January 25, 1077, the feast of the conversion of St. Paul. Chronicles tell that Henry had appeared before the castle of Canossa in penitent dress and after three days Gregory lifted his excommunication, only five days before the deadline set by the opposing princes. The image of Henry going to Canossa in an attitude of humble penitence is essentially based on one main source, Lambert of Hersfeld, a strong supporter of the pope and a member of the opposition nobility. The penance was, in any case, a formal act, performed by Henry, and one that the pope most likely could not refuse; it appears today as a clever diplomatic maneuver, which provided the emperor with freedom of action while limiting that of the pope. However, it is certain that, in the long run, this event inflicted a severe blow to the position of the German Empire.

The absolution from excommunication, however, was the outcome of a protracted negotiation and occurred only upon the king's assumption of precise commitments.

Gregory VII asserted supreme papal authority over secular power, vesting in him the authority to establish the conditions under which it could exercise power and under which subjects were called upon to obey him. It was with reluctance that Gregory accepted repentance because, by granting absolution, the diet of princes at Augsburg, in which he had reasonable hopes of acting as arbiter, would have become useless or, if it had succeeded in convening, would have changed his character completely. It was, however, impossible to deny the penitent a return to the Church, and Gregory's religious obligations overrode political interests.

The removal of the condemnation did not imply true reconciliation, and there was no basis for the resolution of the great issue at stake: that of investiture. A new conflict was inevitable for the simple fact that Henry IV, of course, considered the sentence of deposition annulled along with the sentence of excommunication; while Gregory, for his part, was intent on reserving his freedom of action and gave no cue on the issue to Canossa.

The anti-King and the Emperor's second excommunication

While Henry IV was still in Italy and negotiating his absolution from excommunication, the German nobles who opposed him ganged up against him. Not only did they persist in their policy even after the absolution but went so far as to install, on March 15, 1077, a rival king in the person of Duke Rudolf of Swabia. The papal legates present at the election were apparently neutral, and Gregory himself tried to maintain this attitude in the following years. This position was facilitated by the equivalence that the two factions displayed at the time, each seeking a decisive advantage that would bring the pope to their side. However, such neutrality soon cost him the loss of much of the trust from both contenders.

In June, Henry excluded Rudolph from the Empire and began to confront him in what is commonly known as the Great Revolt of the Saxons immediately suffering two defeats: on August 7, 1078 at the Battle of Mellrichstadt and on January 27, 1080 at the Battle of Flarchheim. As a result, Gregory chose to side with the victor, the anti-king Rudolf, abandoning the wait-and-see policy. On March 7, 1080, he again pronounced for the deposition and excommunication of Henry.

However, the second papal condemnation did not have the same consequences as the previous one. The more experienced king faced the confrontation with the pontiff with great vigor, refusing to recognize the condemnation by claiming its illegality. He convened a council of the German episcopate in Brixen; Hugh Candide was again the protagonist, accusing the pontiff of being a murderer and a heretic. On June 26, 1080, Henry IV declared

Gregory deposed and appointed Archbishop Guibert of Ravenna as the new pontiff. At the battle on the Elster the following October 14, Rudolph was shot dead.

Meanwhile, the pontiff had met in Ceprano with the Norman duke Robert Guiscard, whose excommunication of 1075 had been lifted, where a treaty was concluded. By this the title of duke was returned to Robert and the Holy See definitively renounced the former territories of the Byzantine empire in southern Italy, while acquiring a militarily strong ally. The Normans therefore became vassals of the papacy, required to make a periodic payment and, above all, to guarantee aid to the Church in "maintaining, acquiring and defending the *regalia of* St. Peter and its possessions [...] to maintain surely and honorably the Roman papacy."

The emperor in Italy and the sack of Rome

In 1081 Henry, on the strength of the victory he had achieved the previous year over Rudolphus, opened the conflict against Gregory in Italy. He then crossed the Alps and in February 1082 reached the gates of Rome, where he held fruitless negotiations. Henry then attempted to use force by setting fire to the Vatican basilica, but failing in his attempt he decided to fall back to Sabina. With the new year, 1083, Henry returned to the attack and succeeded in breaching the walls of the Lion City, forcing Gregory VII to take refuge in the Castel Sant'Angelo. The king remained in Rome until late autumn, then returned home confident that he had the capital of Western Christendom in his own hands. In the following months, Gregory VII convened a synod of bishops in which Henry was not explicitly excommunicated, but rather "all those" who had prevented bishops close to the Holy See from taking part.

Learning of this, Henry re-entered Rome on March 21, 1084. The whole city was in his hands except Castel Sant'Angelo where Pope Gregory continued to resist. Most of the cardinals, however, had turned their backs on the pontiff, and at a council in St. Peter's convened for March 24 to judge the pope, Gregory VII was excommunicated and deposed. So at St. John Lateran Guibert of Ravenna was elected as his successor, taking the name Clement III. On March 31 Clement crowned Henry IV as emperor.

After several months of siege and fruitless negotiations, Gregory VII sent for Robert of Altavilla, Duke of Apulia and Calabria, to come to the rescue. Upon hearing the news, the antipope Clement III and Henry IV moved away from Rome. Arriving in Rome, the Normans, after a brief siege, liberated Pope Gregory and then set about a devastation of the Urbe, making themselves responsible for plunder and destruction worse than that of the Gothic sack of 410 and the Lansquenet sack of 1527. Hugh of Flavigny, recounting those events, spoke of great misdeeds, rape and violence, carried out against the guilty and the innocent.

The catastrophe that had befallen the Eternal City was the final blow that finally sank the bond between Gregory VII and Rome. In the eyes of the Romans he represented nothing more than the man who had drawn a series of misfortunes upon them. Gregory understood that when the Norman troops returned to their territories, the Romans would plot their revenge against him. He therefore decided, in June 1084, to leave Rome in the wake of the Hauteville troops and set out for the Mezzogiorno. Rome had been left undefended: it was easy for Clement III, pending the development of events, to retake possession of the city.

Exile in Salerno and the last years

Gregory VII spent the last years of his life in Salerno, a city that was part of the dominions of Robert of Altavilla. He consecrated the cathedral and toward the end of the year convened his last council, in which he renewed the excommunication against Henry IV and Clement III.

Death and burial

On May 25, 1085, Gregory died following an illness that had struck him earlier in the year. He was buried in pontifical robes in a third-century Roman sarcophagus. The Romans and several of his most trusted supporters had abandoned him, and his faithful in Germany had dwindled to a small number. Carved on his tomb was the phrase *Dilexi justitiam et odivi iniquitatem propterea morior in exilio* ("I have loved justice and hated iniquity: therefore I die in exile"), which tradition has it that he himself had uttered at the point of death.

Worship

He was canonized in 1606 by Pope Paul V while the liturgical memorial was set by Pope Benedict XIII on May 25.

In 1954, at the behest of Pope Pius XII, his body was first transported for a few days to Rome for public display and then was rearranged in Salerno Cathedral in a silver reliquary, where it remains to this day. In 1985 his body was the subject of a canonical survey, with examination of his bone remains, which advanced his birth to 1010-1015 and allowed for a comprehensive anthropological and paleopathological study carried out by paleopathologist Gino Fornaciari of the University of Pisa.

Impact of the "Gregorian reform"

Despite Gregory's eventual defeat, the so-called "Gregorian reform" and the struggle for investiture greatly increased the power of the papacy, which was no longer subservient to the emperor, coming to conquer that "*libertas ecclesiae*" long claimed. During his pontificate, "the concept of the absolute primacy of the pope of Rome in the sphere of the church" was affirmed with unprecedented evidence, so much so that the ecclesiastical organizational structure changed from a horizontal to a pyramidal model with the pontiff "the sole and undisputed summit." In addition, the Holy See found itself at the head of vassal states, owing an annual tribute, consisting mainly of the Norman principalities of southern

Italy, the Marque of Spain in southern France, and principalities located eastward in the Dalmatian coastal regions, Hungary and Poland. The powerful Cluniac order also grew even stronger, and at the same time new orders such as the Camaldolese, Carthusians and Cistercians, all supporters of the Reformation and the papacy, emerged.

The political and economic power of these monastic orders, particularly first the Cluniac and later the Cistercian, was such that it ended up directly influencing the decisions of princes. At its peak, the church came to direct the social policy of the Christian West, of which the beginning of the Crusades is a clear example. However, in keeping with the traditional Christian division between Caesar and God, it came to the sharing of power between papacy and secular authorities. On the other hand, the sustained economic growth of which the West was a protagonist did not delay the emergence of a bourgeois class that gradually went on to establish itself as a new force within the tripartite system typical of feudal society, previously composed only of clergy, nobility and people. The crisis of imperial power, which lasted for a long time until the advent of authoritarian emperors such as Frederick Barbarossa, contributed, according to many historians, to the emergence of nation states and, in northern Italy, medieval communes. Finally, it has also been pointed out that the Gregorian reform, and more generally the reform of the 11th century, contributed to the phenomenon known as the "12th century renaissance."

Gregory and his "crusade"

From the mid-11th century, a Gregorian thought of Christian reconquest and liberation of the Catholic Church took shape. As early as 1074 Gregory VII had conceived of a crusade project, articulated as a response to Islamic expansion. Indeed, following the defeat of Byzantine troops at the Battle of Manzicerta in 1071 by the Seljuk Turks, the Byzantine Empire had lost much of Syria, leaving an open door for the Muslim people to Anatolia.

In the face of this situation, Gregory saw this progress of the Turks at the expense of Eastern Christendom as "the sign of the devil's action" determined to destroy Christendom, ravaging it from within with heresy and the corruption of ecclesiastics. This demonization of the "Saracens" by Christian clerics was the fruit of a rhetorical construction adverse to Islam that existed from its beginnings and of which Isidore of Seville and the Apocalypse of Pseudo-Methodius are considered the precursors.

In reaction to these events, Pope Gregory went so far as to consider personally leading an army to Jerusalem in aid of the Eastern Christians. With this in mind he wrote, on February 12, 1074, to several princes to put themselves "at the service of St. Peter" by offering him the military assistance they owed him and had promised him. The following March 1 he returned to this project with a letter addressed to "all those who wish to defend the Christian faith." On December 7 of that year, Gregory reiterated his intentions in a letter to Henry IV, in which he evoked the suffering of Christians by informing the emperor that he was ready to go in person to the Holy Sepulcher in Jerusalem at the head of an army of 50,000 men. A week later, he again addressed all his faithful to urge them to go to the aid of the Christians of the East to fight the infidels. Finally, in a letter dated January 22, 1075, Gregory expressed his deep discouragement to Hugh of Cluny by deploring all the "misfortunes" that were overwhelming the Church: the Greek schism in the East, heresy and simony in the West, the Turkish wave in the Near East, and, finally, the inertia of European princes in the face of all this.

This "crusade" project was never carried out when Gregory VII was alive; in fact, the ideas of holy war had not yet unanimously convinced the Christians of the West, but were later revived by Pope Urban II, who, at the Council of Clermont in 1095, gave impetus to what would be known as the First Crusade.

Relations with Christian kingdoms

Although by the mid-9th century the geographic horizon of the papacy had expanded to far beyond Rome, Gregory VII's pontificate is also remembered for the intense and complex relations he undertook with the rulers of Europe; his correspondence reached Poland, Bohemia and Russia. He wrote in friendly terms to the Muslim king of Mauritania and tried unsuccessfully to bring the Armenian Church into communion with Rome. Gregory VII, however, did not travel much during his pontificate, preferring to rely on papal legates of his own choosing, such as Hugh of Cluny, Hugh of Die, and Amatus of Oleron, to whom he conferred very extensive delegations in their missions.

Gregory was particularly interested in the Eastern Orthodox Churches. The schism between Rome and the Byzantine Church was a severe blow to him, and he worked at length to restore previous fraternal relations by maintaining contact with Emperor Michael VII. When news of the Arab attack on the Eastern Christians reached Rome and the Byzantine emperor's political embarrassment increased, Gregory conceived plans for a major military expedition and urged the faithful to participate in the reconquest of the Basilica of the Holy Sepulcher.

In relations with other European states, Gregory's intervention turned out to be much more moderate than his policy toward the German princes. The clash with the Holy Roman Empire on the one hand left him little energy to deal with similar clashes simultaneously and on the other had special features, including the imperial claim to elect and depose popes. Philip I of France, with his practice of simony and the violence of his actions against the Church, also provoked a threat of punitive measures: excommunication, deposition and interdiction appeared imminent in 1074. Gregory, however, avoided translating threats into action, although the king's attitude showed no change.

In England, William the Conqueror also obtained benefits from this state of affairs. He felt so safe that he interfered in an autocratic way with the administration of the Church, forbidding bishops to travel to Rome, making appointments of bishops and abbots, and remaining imperturbable when the pope lectured him on his views about church-state relations, or when he forbade him to trade or ordered him to recognize himself as a vassal of the Apostolic See. Gregory had no power to compel the English king to a change in his ecclesiastical policies, so he chose to ignore what he could not approve of, and even found it appropriate to reassure him of his paternal affection.

Consistories for the creation of new cardinals

Pope Gregory VII during his pontificate created 31 cardinals during nine separate consistories.

Apostolic succession

The apostolic succession of Gregory VII is:

- Cardinal Anselm of Lucca (1073)

- Archbishop Hugh of Die (1074)

- Bishop Bernardo Guillén (1076)

- Cardinal Bruno di Segni, O.S.B.Cas. (1080)

- Bishop Hugh of Grenoble (1080)

- Bishop Didier (1082)

- Bishop Bernard (1083)

URBANVS . VII . ROMANVS . PON . OPT . MAX .

Other books by United Library

https://campsite.bio/unitedlibrary